To:

From:

20th Century Memories

A LOOK BACK THROUGH THE DECADES
1900–1999

By Barbara & Kenneth Leish

PETER PAUPER PRESS, INC.
White Plains, New York

Designed by La Shae V. Ortiz

Picture credits appear on page 128

Copyright © 2011
Peter Pauper Press, Inc.
202 Mamaroneck Avenue
White Plains, NY 10601
ISBN 978-1-4413-0635-7
Printed in China
7 6 5 4 3 2 1

Visit us at www.peterpauper.com

20th Century Memories

A LOOK BACK THROUGH THE DECADES

1900–1999

Contents

Introduction 6

Remembering the **1900s** 8

Remembering the **1910s** 20

Remembering the **1920s** 32

Remembering the **1930s** 44

Remembering the **1940s** 56

Remembering the **1950s** 68

Remembering the **1960s** 80

Remembering the **1970s** 92

Remembering the **1980s** 104

Remembering the **1990s** 116

Picture Credits 128

Introduction
Remembering the Twentieth Century

If Rip Van Winkle had fallen asleep in 1900 and awakened in 1999, there wouldn't be much he would have recognized. Instead of horse-drawn buggies on muddy roads, he'd see sleek automobiles speeding along multi-lane highways. He'd see people who looked like they were talking to themselves while holding strange objects to their ears, and others carrying rectangular cases that connected them instantly to faraway places. And if Rip

looked up to the sky, he'd see winged tubes that carried people around the globe in hours, rather than the weeks such trips had taken in 1900.

As Rip learned more about his new world, he'd discover that humans could travel to the moon, save lives by transplanting human organs, and produce energy by splitting the atom. He'd also learn, to his disappointment, that the human race had not yet ended war nor wiped out poverty.

All in all, the twentieth century was remarkable. And you, who lived rather than slept through it, can take a nostalgic trip back through the decades with *20th Century Memories*, reliving the events, fads and fancies, firsts and favorites, and the social changes and landmark achievements of each year.

Enjoy!

Remembering the
1900s

America entered the new century full of *confidence and optimism. Its quick victory in the Spanish-American War of 1898 had made the United States a world power and given it control of Puerto Rico, the Philippines, and Guam.*

There were about 76 million Americans in 1900. Sixty percent lived on farms or in small towns, but immigrants from Europe were swelling the populations of the nation's cities. New inventions and technological advances were rapidly changing the way people lived: There were already some 8,000 automobiles registered in the country, although there were as yet only 144 miles of paved road. It was a time of prosperity and innovation, a time when anything seemed possible.

In 1909, onlookers shouted "Get a horse!," when President William Howard Taft and his wife rode out of the White House grounds in a "steam snorter." It was the first official presidential automobile.

1900

The **Kodak Brownie**, the first inexpensive camera—it costs just $1—quickly makes the U.S. a nation of amateur photographers.

- Candy-lovers are delighted by another new product, **Hershey's milk chocolate bar.**

- Congress officially declares **Hawaii** a United States Territory. American sugar planters there had asked the U.S. to annex the islands.

- The average **life expectancy for Americans is 49.2 years.** The average worker earns 22 cents an hour, rib roast costs 10 cents a pound, and butter 25 cents a pound. A man can buy a worsted suit for $7.

- Frank L. Baum's *The Wonderful Wizard of Oz* is published, introducing readers to Dorothy, the Tin Woodman, the Cowardly Lion, and the Scarecrow.

- **William McKinley,** a Republican from Ohio, is re-elected president in November. The vice president-elect is Theodore Roosevelt, the young, exuberant governor of New York.

- Carrie Nation and members of the **anti-liquor temperance movement** vandalize saloons in Kansas.

1901

- Oil gushes from a well at **Spindletop Mound** near Beaumont, Texas. It is the first oil strike in Texas and sets off a mad rush for "black gold" in the nation's largest state.

- Britain's **Queen Victoria** dies at the age of 81 after a reign of 63 years.

- An important medical breakthrough occurs when an American neurosurgeon, **Harvey Cushing**, introduces an inflatable cuff, the first practical device for measuring blood pressure.

President McKinley, 25th president of the United States, is shot by an anarchist on September 6 and dies eight days later. Theodore Roosevelt becomes, at 42, the youngest man ever to serve as president.

President McKinley with his wife Ida Saxton McKinley.

- Roosevelt is the first president to invite an African-American—the distinguished educator **Booker T. Washington**—to dine with his family at the White House. The invitation results in a storm of criticism from people opposed to integration of the races.

1902

- The first post-season college football game, sponsored by the **Tournament of Roses** Association, takes place in Pasadena, California. The University of Michigan beats Stanford, 49–0. Not until 1923 will the annual event become known as the Rose Bowl game.

- Willis Carrier develops the first **air conditioner**, designed for businesses and factories. The first home units will not be introduced until 1929.

- The **U.S. Army** exchanges its blue uniforms for olive drab ones. During the Spanish-American War, officers realized that blue made too good a target for the enemy.

- **James Cash Penney** opens his first store in Kemmerer, Wyoming, in a one-room wooden building. He and his family live in the attic above the store.

"In the Good Old Summer Time," a song by Ren Shields and George Evans, sells a million copies of sheet music in a 12-month period.

1903

Helen Keller's inspirational autobiography, *The Story of My Life*, is published. She lost her sight and hearing when she was 19 months old, but learned to write and speak and graduated with honors from Radcliffe College.

- The **first baseball World Series** is won by the Boston Americans, who defeat the Pittsburgh Pirates 5 games to 3. The Americans change their name to the Red Sox in 1908.

- The first movie western, ***The Great Train Robbery***, thrills audiences. The highlight of the 12-minute-long silent film is a scene in which a desperado points his gun directly at the audience and fires.

- The **Wright Brothers** make the first powered, controlled flight in a heavier-than-air plane. The flight, on the dunes at Kitty Hawk, North Carolina, lasts just 12 seconds.

- The **automobile windshield wiper** is invented by Mary Anderson, an Alabama woman, during a visit to New York City.

Popular gifts for children this year: **Teddy bears**, stuffed animals inspired by President Roosevelt's decision to spare a bear during a hunting expedition, and the first **Crayola** product, a box of 8 crayons selling for 5 cents.

13

1904

The ***General Slocum***, a paddle steamer carrying church members to a picnic, catches fire on New York City's East River. More than a thousand people die in the disaster.

- St. Louis hosts a World's Fair, The Louisiana Purchase Exposition, which inspires the song, **"Meet Me in St. Louis."** Fair-goers enjoy a new treat, **ice-cream cones**.

- New York City opens its **first subway line**. It extends for nine miles. The nation's first subway had opened in Boston in 1897.

- New products introduced include **Campbell's Pork and Beans**, French's Cream Salad Mustard, Colgate Ribbon Dental Cream, and Dr Pepper soda. The Gillette razor is patented.

- **Cy Young** of the Boston Americans pitches the first perfect game of baseball's modern era, facing 27 batters in 9 innings.

- **Teddy Roosevelt** easily wins November's presidential election.

1905

- Four Chicago businessmen form the **first Rotary Club**. Weekly meetings rotate among the members' offices—hence the name.

- Eighteen-year-old **Ty Cobb** launches his long career with the Detroit Tigers. By the time he retires in 1928, he will have batted over .300 in 23 straight seasons and achieved a lifetime batting average of .367.

- Frank Epperson, an 11-year-old from San Francisco, **invents the popsicle**, when a fruit drink he leaves out overnight on the porch (with a stirrer in it) freezes. He calls it the Epsicle and 18 years later patents it.

- Both the Pennsylvania Railroad and the New York Central Railroad inaugurate **18-hour train service** between New York and Chicago.

Madame C. J. Walker,

the entrepreneurial daughter of former slaves, begins selling hair and beauty products door-to-door. The business will make her one of the first women millionaires in America.

1906

- In a sensational crime, eminent architect **Stanford White**, who designed the Washington Square Arch (pictured on right) in New York City, among other buildings, is shot and killed at a party in Madison Square Garden by millionaire Harry Kendall Thaw, whose young wife is White's former lover.

- Teddy Roosevelt becomes the first American to win the **Nobel Peace Prize**, awarded for his role in ending the war between Russia and Japan in 1905.

- San Francisco is struck by a **devastating earthquake**. Fires rage for days, as many as 3,000 people are killed, and 250,000 are left homeless.

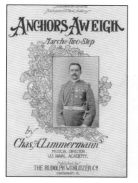

- Upton Sinclair's novel *The Jungle*, an exposé of the meat-packing industry, helps spur Congress to pass the Pure Food and Drugs Act.

"Anchors Aweigh" is written as a football fight song for the U.S. Naval Academy, and is played for the first time at the Army–Navy football game in Philadelphia.

1907

- The luxury retail store **Neiman Marcus opens** in Dallas. Its initial stock of dresses, furs, gowns, coats, and hats is snapped up within weeks.

- **Florenz Ziegfeld** stages his first Broadway extravaganza. The elaborately costumed show-girls in the *Ziegfeld Follies* are notably slim, which is widely considered a sign of poor health.

- To show the world that the United States has a powerful navy, President Roosevelt sends the **Great White Fleet**—a squadron of 16 battleships—on an around-the-world tour.

- Oklahoma—incorporating **Oklahoma Territory** and what remains of Indian Territory—is admitted to the Union as the 46th state.

- In December two **devastating coal-mine explosions**—one in West Virginia, the other in Pennsylvania—kill more than 600 miners.

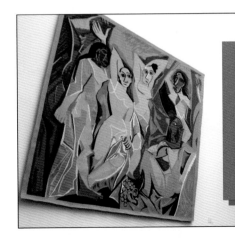

Picasso launches the Cubist movement with his painting *Les Demoiselles d'Avignon*, a work in which traditional linear perspective is replaced by flat planes.

- Eager for every American to be able to afford a car, **Henry Ford introduces** the Model T, which sells for $850. In the first year alone, more than 10,000 are sold.

- New York City's Board of Aldermen pass the **Sullivan Ordinance**, making it illegal for women to smoke in public.

- **The Dow Jones Industrial Average** ends the year at 86.15, up from 58.75 a year earlier.

- Tea and coffee merchant Thomas Sullivan invents the **tea bag** when he begins wrapping tea samples in tiny silk bags. Customers discover that the bags can go directly into boiling water.

- **"Mutt and Jeff"** debuts in William Randolph Hearst's *San Francisco Examiner*. It is the first comic strip to appear daily with the same recurring figures.

"Take Me Out to the Ball Game," written by two men who have never been to a major league game, becomes one of the most popular songs of the year—and then of the century.

1909

William Howard Taft (seated above with his wife, Helen "Nellie") becomes the country's 27th president. He will later serve as Chief Justice of the Supreme Court—the only American to hold both offices.

- In response to impassioned race riots in 1908 in Springfield, Illinois, 60 black and white leaders meet in New York City and form the **National Association for the Advancement of Colored People** (NAACP).

- **Robert E. Peary** reaches the North Pole. He is accompanied by Matthew Henson, his longtime traveling partner and the first African-American to reach the pole.

- The **Sixteenth Amendment** to the Constitution, authorizing Congress to impose income taxes, is submitted to the states for ratification.

- **Prohibition** comes to North Carolina, which becomes the first state in the nation to ban alcoholic beverages by popular vote.

Remembering the **1910s**

In the 1910s, America continued to grow and prosper. But many people were discontented, and they marched and demonstrated in support of their causes. Increasing numbers of women were demanding the right to vote. Workers were striking against unfair wages and unsafe working conditions, temperance supporters were urging the government to ban all alcoholic drinks. And when World War I began in Europe in 1914, some Americans marched to urge President Wilson to keep the nation out of the war.

In 1917, the U.S. did join the conflict in Europe. With more than two million U.S. soldiers in France, Americans studied maps of France to find places they had never heard of (Château-Thierry, Saint-Mihiel, the Argonne Forest), but which are now the final resting places of more than 115,000 American young men.

The British ship, RMS Lusitania, *is sunk by a German submarine.*

1910

- **William D. Boyce**, a Chicago publisher, founds the Boy Scouts of America, adopting the motto "Be Prepared."

- The first public radio broadcast features tenor **Enrico Caruso**, singing from the Metropolitan Opera in New York.

- The **U.S. population**, swelled by the arrival of almost 9 million immigrants in the past decade, is now 92 million.

- **Jack Johnson**, an African-American boxer, defeats former champ James J. Jeffries, a white man, in a fight for the world heavyweight championship in the 15th round. Race riots break out in some U.S. cities as a result.

- Some astronomers predict that the fiery tail of **Halley's Comet** will poison people on Earth when the comet passes by this year. A minor panic ensues, with some people buying bogus "comet pills" to counter the effects of the poisonous gas. But the comet causes no harm.

Two **great writers**, American Mark Twain (shown wearing his Oxford University robe after he got an honorary degree) and Russian Leo Tolstoy, die.

LADIES WAIST & DRESSMAKERS UNION OCAL 25 W MOURN OUR LOSS

A fire at the **Triangle Shirtwaist Factory** in New York kills 146 young immigrant women and spurs demands for improved health and safety conditions for workers. At left union members gather to protest and mourn the loss of life in the fire.

- The Supreme Court orders the breakup of **John D. Rockefeller's** Standard Oil, a giant monopoly.

- **Pilot Calbraith Rodgers** makes the first airplane trip from New York to California. He stops for plane repairs about 70 times during the journey, which takes 49 days.

- The first **Indianapolis 500** motor race takes place. The winner's average speed is 74.6 miles per hour.

- **Roald Amundsen**, a Norwegian explorer, is the first man to reach the South Pole.

- Irving Berlin's song **"Alexander's Ragtime Band"** becomes an international hit.

1912

New Mexico and Arizona join the union as the 47th and 48th states.

- The **U.S. sends 2,500 marines to Nicaragua** to help the pro-American government there put down a rebellion.

- **Woodrow Wilson**, a Democrat, is elected President, easily beating incumbent William Howard Taft and Teddy Roosevelt.

- Jim Thorpe, a **Native American, wins gold medals** in both the pentathlon and decathlon at the Olympics in Sweden.

- **Oreo cookies** are introduced, and prizes are included in every **Cracker Jack box** for the first time.

The supposedly unsinkable ocean liner **Titanic** hits an iceberg in the Atlantic and sinks, killing some 1,500 people.

1913

- The **16th amendment** to the U.S. Constitution, approving a national income tax, is ratified. At first, the highest tax rate is 7% on incomes over $500,000.

The 60-story Woolworth building in New York opens; it is the tallest structure in the world. Also new is **Grand Central Terminal** (pictured here), the world's largest railroad station.

- **Henry Ford** introduces the **assembly line** at his plant in Highland Park, Michigan. Now a Model T can be assembled in six hours.

- The first **electric refrigerator** for homes goes on the market.

- American **Francis Ouimet** upsets top British golfers and wins the U.S. Open, sparking a surge in golf's popularity.

Art lovers attending the Armory Show in New York City are **shocked** by the **Cubist** and post-Impressionist paintings of Picasso, **Kandinsky** (shown at right), Duchamp, and other tradition-shattering artists.

1914

- **World War I begins** in Europe, pitting Germany and Austria-Hungary against Great Britain, France, and Russia.
- The **Panama Canal opens**. It is estimated that 30,000 people died from disease and accidents during the construction of the canal, which was begun by France and completed by the U.S.

The Perils of Pauline, a silent movie serial starring Pearl White, thrills audiences. In each of the 20 weekly episodes, which are 20 to 30 minutes long, the heroine faces heartless villains who put her in jeopardy.

- In what becomes known as **The Ludlow Massacre**, striking miners are shot and their homes burned down by mining company forces and National Guard members in Ludlow, Colorado. The strikers fail to achieve higher wages or safer working conditions.
- The **last passenger pigeon** dies in a zoo in Cincinnati. Once the most populous bird on Earth, billions of them flourished in the 1800s, but hunters decimated them and settlers destroyed their habitats.

President Woodrow Wilson officially proclaims the second Sunday of May as **Mother's Day**.

1915

A German submarine sinks the RMS *Lusitania*, a British passenger ship, off the coast of Ireland. About 1,200 people die, including 123 Americans. As a result, anti-German sentiment soars in the U.S.

- *The Birth of a Nation*, an epic Civil War film by director D. W. Griffith that cost an unprecedented $110,000 to produce, is hailed by some critics as the greatest achievement of the silent cinema. But it is also condemned for its racist portrayal of black people.

- The **first transcontinental telephone call** is made by Alexander Graham Bell in New York City to his colleague Thomas Watson in San Francisco.

- **Bayer first markets aspirin in tablet form**, rather than as a powder, and it also becomes available without a prescription.

- U.S. troops occupy **Haiti**, where war between militia groups and warlords has created chaos. Americans would control the island nation until 1934.

American troops under John J. Pershing (on right) enter northern Mexico in pursuit of **Pancho Villa** (middle), a bandit and revolutionary leader who had raided a U.S. border town. This picture was taken before the attack on U.S. soil. General Álvaro Obregon Salido on the left, helped in the Mexican Revolution, and later became President of Mexico in 1920.

- **Margaret Sanger**, an advocate of birth control, opens a family planning clinic in Brooklyn. She is arrested and serves 30 days in jail for distributing obscene material.

- The French air force establishes the **Lafayette Escadrille**, a unit of American pilots who want to fight against the Germans even though the U.S. is not at war. Nine of the Americans will lose their lives in aerial combat.

- Albert Einstein publishes his general **theory of relativity**, which revolutionizes thinking about time, matter, energy, and gravity.

- The **National Park Service** is established.

- Campaigning on the slogan **"He kept us out of war,"** Woodrow Wilson is re-elected president.

1917

Bolshevik revolutionaries (marching in Siberia) **overthrow** the Czarist regime and take control of Russia. Communist party supporters marking the 1917 Revolution (right) hold a poster depicting former Soviet dictator Joseph Stalin and Soviet founder Vladimir Lenin during a rally.

- The United States **purchases** the Danish Virgin Islands: St. Croix, St. John, and St. Thomas.

- The song **"Livery Stable Blues"** is recorded by the all-white Original Dixieland Jazz Band. It sells more than a million copies, greatly increasing the popularity of jazz music.

- **Jeannette Rankin** of Montana becomes the first woman to serve in the U.S. Congress.

- The U.S. uncovers a **German plot** to join with Mexico in an attack against America. After German U-boats sink four American merchant ships in March, President Wilson asks Congress to declare war on Germany.

1918

The U.S. Post Office inaugurates regular **airmail** service between Washington, DC, Philadelphia, and New York. It is a dangerous job for the pilots, who experience many crashes and 16 fatalities before transcontinental service begins in 1920.

A horrible **influenza** pandemic kills an estimated 675,000 Americans and between 20 and 40 million people worldwide.

- Margaret B. Owen of New York City sets a **world typewriting record**: 170 words a minute with no errors on a manual typewriter.

- Nicholas II, the **deposed Russian Czar**, is executed by the Bolsheviks, along with his wife and children. His daughter, Anastasia, is believed to be alive by many.

- **World War I ends.** The Americans play a decisive role in bringing about the German surrender on November 11. United States deaths in combat or from disease are 116,516, and another 204,000 Americans are wounded.

1919

- President Wilson attends the peace conference in France, where the **Treaty of Versailles** inflicts harsh punishments on the defeated Germans. A new world organization, the League of Nations, is established, but the U.S. Congress decides to keep the U.S. out of the League.

- Sports fans are shocked by the revelation that eight members of the **Chicago White Sox** had agreed to lose the 1919 World Series. The disgraced players become known as the Black Sox.

- The **18th amendment** to the Constitution, prohibiting the manufacture, sale, and transportation of all alcoholic drinks, is ratified.

- **Sir Barton** becomes the first horse to win American racing's Triple Crown: the Kentucky Derby, the Preakness Stakes, and the Belmont Stakes.

- Worried that communist **sympathizers** are plotting against the U.S., the government rounds up alleged anarchists and communists and deports them.

In Boston, a huge steel tank holding 2.3 million gallons of **molasses** explodes. A flood of molasses rushes down the streets, drowning horses and people and destroying homes and stores.

Remembering the **1920s**

With the war behind them, Americans threw off constraints. The
pleasure-loving 1920s—aptly named The Roaring Twenties—were marked
by exuberance, brashness, and a flouting of conventions. Young Americans
embraced new styles in clothes, music, and entertainment. Technological
advances in areas such as communication (the radio) and transportation
(cars and planes) opened up new possibilities and freedoms. Jazz, flappers,
the Charleston, bootleg whiskey—all these and more are what make the
1920s one of the most instantly recognized decades in U.S. history.

But the good times ended suddenly and calamitously with the stock market
crash of 1929, which wiped out fortunes, shuttered businesses, and put huge
numbers of people out of work.

President Warren G. Harding with his pet airedale Laddie Boy.

1920

The popular 1920 silent film ***The Flapper*** introduces a new woman to the U.S. With her short skirts, bobbed hair, and independent behavior, the flapper becomes a symbol of the free-spirited 1920s.

- After years of struggle by **women suffragists**, the 19th amendment to the Constitution, granting women the right to vote, is ratified.

- **Nicola Sacco** and **Bartolomeo Vanzetti**, Italian immigrants and anarchists, are arrested in Massachusetts for murder, convicted the next year, and executed in 1927. Many feel they are innocent victims of prejudice.

- For the first time, **the rural population** in the U.S. declines to less than half of the total population of 106,521,537.

- The great racehorse **Man O' War** wins the Preakness and the Belmont Stakes. In 1999 he will be named Horse of the Century.

Warren Harding (shown at left) is elected President. His administration will be remembered for graft and corruption.

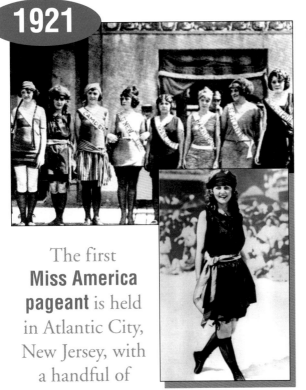

The first **Miss America pageant** is held in Atlantic City, New Jersey, with a handful of contestants.

Margaret Gorman of Washington, DC poses after winning the Miss America title.

- **Black Swan Records**, the first widely circulated label owned by African-Americans and featuring black musicians, is founded in Harlem. Its first big hit is Ethel Waters singing "Down Home Blues."

- More than 90,000 fans pack a Jersey City stadium to watch heavyweight champion **Jack Dempsey** defeat Frenchman Georges Carpentier. It is boxing's first million-dollar gate, and the first fight to be broadcast on radio.

- A year after Prohibition begins, bootleggers are doing a brisk business. Many people drink in secret bars called **speakeasies**, and gangsters fight bloody battles for control of the illegal trade.

Pueblo, Colorado, is heavily damaged when the **Arkansas River floods**. Almost 1,500 die, and property loss is greater than $20 million.

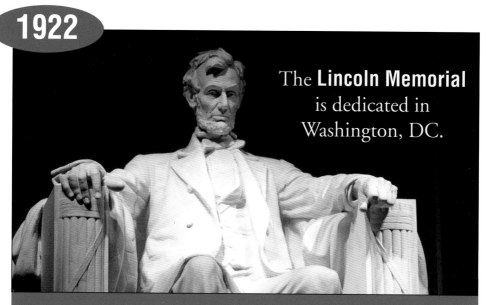

1922

The **Lincoln Memorial** is dedicated in Washington, DC.

- The **Golden Age of radio** has begun. Westinghouse markets the first pre-assembled radio. A front-page *Variety* headline proclaims, "Radio Sweeping Country: 1,000,000 Sets in Use."

- The Czech playwright **Karel Câpek's** play *R.U.R.*, which has its U.S. premiere in New York, introduces the term "robot."

- New York postal authorities destroy several hundred copies of **James Joyce's** novel *Ulysses*, which is banned from the U.S. as obscene. The Modern Library in 1999 will select it as the best novel of the century.

- The English archaeologist Howard Carter discovers **King Tut's tomb** in Egypt's Valley of the Kings.

1923

- After a resurgent **Ku Klux Klan** steps up its violent activities in Oklahoma, the governor places part of the state under martial law.

- The first issue of the weekly magazine *Time* is published. Founders Henry Luce and Briton Hadden conceive it as a concise news source for busy men.

- B.F. Goodrich coins the word **"zipper"** to describe the sound made by the closers on the rubber galoshes his company sells.

President Harding dies of a heart attack, and Vice President **Calvin Coolidge**, shown above in an artist's rendering, is sworn in as President at his home in Plymouth, Vermont.

- The Senate begins an investigation of **Teapot Dome**, one of the worst scandals of the Harding administration, involving bribes to allow drilling for oil at Teapot Dome, Wyoming.

- The 1923 Broadway musical *Runnin' Wild* features James P. Johnson's song **"Charleston."** The dance of the same name becomes all the rage.

1924

- Crazes that sweep the country include the Chinese game **mah-jongg** and dance marathons.

- The **Immigrations Act of 1924** severely restricts immigration from southern and eastern Europe and bans immigration from East Asia and India.

- Two privileged Chicago teenagers, **Nathan Leopold and Richard Loeb, kidnap and murder** a 14-year-old acquaintance to see if they could commit the perfect crime. They are caught, convicted, and sentenced to life in prison.

- The Notre Dame football team, led by a backfield nicknamed the **"Four Horsemen"** and coached by Knute Rockne, wins the national college football championship.

Calvin Coolidge is elected to a full term as president. He is the first president to address the nation on radio. Some 5 million people listen.

Calvin Coolidge and his wife, Grace, on the platform of their private car at Pennsylvania Station.

1925

- The Yankees' **Lou Gehrig** begins his 15-season streak of 2,130 consecutive games, a record that stands for 70 years.

- **Teacher John Scopes** is tried in Tennessee for breaking a state law by teaching Darwin's theory of evolution. Despite Clarence Darrow's defense, Scopes is found guilty and fined $100.

- **F. Scott Fitzgerald's** novel *The Great Gatsby* captures the dreams and excesses of the Jazz Age, a term Fitzgerald coins for the 1920s.

Louis Armstrong.

- The first volume of **Hitler's** *Mein Kampf* is published. Volume 2 appears next year.

- Congress creates the **numbered Interstate Highway system**. North-south highways are given odd numbers; east-west highways, even numbers.

The legendary jazzman **Louis Armstrong** releases "My Heart," his first record under his own name.

1926

The Sun Also Rises, **Ernest Hemingway's** novel about disillusioned American expatriates living in Europe, introduces a literary style that becomes widely imitated.

- Robert Goddard, the **father of American rocketry**, launches the first liquid-fuel rocket in Massachusetts. In 1920 Goddard suggested that a rocket could someday reach the moon.

- **Langston Hughes publishes** his first book of poems, *The Weary Blues*. Hughes is a leader of the Harlem Renaissance, a literary movement that celebrates African-American life.

- New York City gets its **first outdoor miniature golf course**—built on the roof of a skyscraper in the financial district. Soon the city has some 150 rooftop courses.

Winnie-the-Pooh is published. A.A. Milne has written the stories for his son, Christopher Robin, whose stuffed-animal collection includes Eeyore, Piglet, Tigger, Kanga, and Roo.

1927

Babe Ruth hits 60 home runs, setting a record that holds until 1961.

- **Charles Lindbergh** makes the first solo nonstop flight across the Atlantic. The trip takes 33 and a half hours and turns Lindbergh into an international hero.
- The Nashville radio program **"WSM Barn Dance"** changes its name to "Grand Ole Opry."
- The **Holland Tunnel**, an engineering marvel connecting New Jersey and New York under the mile-wide Hudson River, is completed.
- In a flood of biblical proportions, the **Mississippi River overflows its banks**, swamping millions of acres from Illinois to Louisiana and forcing more than half a million people from their homes.

Al Jolson sings and talks in *The Jazz Singer*, the first feature-length movie with synchronized sound and some spoken dialogue. By 1930, most of the nation's theaters have converted to sound.

Babe Ruth (on left) with Lou Gehrig.

Mickey, as designed by German toymaker Schucco.

Mickey Mouse stars in his first cartoon, "Steamboat Willie," which is also Walt Disney's first animated cartoon with synchronized sound.

- Eugene O'Neill wins his **third Pulitzer Prize** for his play *Strange Interlude*. O'Neill will go on to win the Nobel Prize for literature in 1936.

- Alexander Fleming, a British scientist, **discovers penicillin**.

- Grocery **shoppers can now buy** Rice Krispies, Velveeta cheese, Peter Pan peanut butter, and Reese's Peanut Butter Cups.

A Fleer Chewing Gum Company accountant, Walter E. Diemer, invents Dubble Bubble Gum.

- **Herbert Hoover is elected president**, easily defeating Al Smith, a New York Catholic whose religion and opposition to Prohibition make him an unpopular candidate.

1929

Hollywood holds the **first Academy Awards** ceremony. Emil Jannings and Janet Gaynor win statuettes—which later become known as Oscars—for Best Actor and Actress.

- Almost **23 million cars** are on the roads, and car ownership has now become commonplace.

- Ernest Lawrence, a physics professor at the University of California at Berkeley, **invents the cyclotron**, a device that makes the study of the atom possible.

- The **Madame Alexander doll** makes her debut and surpasses the Raggedy Ann doll in popularity.

- On October 29, the stock market crashes, ushering in a long economic depression. The day becomes known as "**Black Tuesday.**"

Remembering the **1930s**

Seldom has the contrast between two decades been so stark. *The anything-goes Twenties were followed by the Depression Thirties. Rather than worrying about how to get an alcoholic drink, many Americans now worried about how to get their next meal.*

But American optimism, enthusiasm, and innovation re-emerged as President Franklin D. Roosevelt restored confidence and conditions slowly began to improve. People took pleasure in the accomplishments of their heroes (Charles Lindbergh, Babe Ruth, Jesse Owens), and marveled at the new evidence of American know-how (the Empire State Building, Boulder Dam, frozen foods, increased life expectancies). And they knew that there was no limit to the wonders that science and technology would reveal or create in the future.

The National League All-Star team in Chicago, Illinois.

Two New York City landmarks open:
The **George Washington Bridge** (above) and the 1,250-foot
Empire State Building, the world's tallest structure to date.

- **"The Star-Spangled Banner"** is officially designated as the U.S. national anthem by Congress.

- Gangster **Al Capone** is convicted and jailed on charges of income-tax evasion.

- Jacob Schick sells the **first electric razor** for $25.

- The Nevada legislature votes to **legalize gambling** in the state.

- **Japan invades** Manchuria in China.

1932

Comedian **Jack Benny**
begins his weekly
radio show.

- **Thousands of jobless World War I** veterans march on Washington, DC, demanding payment of a bonus they say Congress had promised them. The men are dispersed by U.S. troops, who attack them with gas, clubs, and bayonets.

- Americans are stunned by the **kidnapping of aviator Charles Lindbergh's 20-month-old son** from the family's home. Two months later, the baby's body is found. Eventually a carpenter, Bruno Hauptmann, will be convicted of the murder and executed.

- **The unemployment rate reaches** 23.6%, and stocks have lost 80% of their value. The average family income is $1,500, down 40% from what it was before the Depression.

- **Franklin Delano Roosevelt**, the governor of New York, is elected President in a landslide. He carries 42 of the 48 states.

1933

Baseball holds its **first All-Star game**, which the American League wins, thanks to a homer by Babe Ruth. In another sports milestone, the National Football League has its first championship game, won by the Chicago Bears.

- **Adolf Hitler becomes chancellor** of Germany, and the Nazi party takes control of the country.

- **Frances Perkins**, the new Secretary of Labor, is the first woman ever to serve in a president's cabinet.

- **Life expectancy for Americans** is now 63.3 years, up 16 years since 1900.

- **Two amendments to the U.S. Constitution are ratified.** The 20th amendment moves the inaugural date for presidents to January from March, and the 21st ends the prohibition of alcoholic drinks.

Crowds gather as kegs of beer, now legal, are unloaded in front of a restaurant.

1934

The **first Masters Tournament** is held at the Augusta National Golf Club in Georgia.

- **Gangster John Dillinger** (Public Enemy Number 1) is killed by the FBI as he leaves a Chicago movie theater. In Louisiana, federal agents kill bank robbers Bonnie Parker and Clyde Barrow.

- The **terrible drought** that has devastated the south-central states grows worse. Winds blow tons of dried-out topsoil for hundreds of miles. Many "dust bowl" families leave their homes and farms.

- Congress establishes the **Securities and Exchange Commission (SEC)** to oversee the stock market.

A Federal penitentiary opens on **Alcatraz**, an island in San Francisco Bay. The prison becomes known as "The Rock."

1935

Americans build houses and hotels on Boardwalk for the first time when the board game *Monopoly* is introduced and becomes an instant hit.

- **Alcoholics Anonymous** is founded in Akron, Ohio.

- **Major league baseball plays its first night game** in Cincinnati, and the Heisman Memorial Trophy for the outstanding college football player of the year is awarded for the first time.

- The DuPont Corporation patents a **new synthetic fiber**, nylon, which will become the most popular material for women's stockings.

- Two major new programs from the Roosevelt Administration are **Social Security** and the Works Progress Administration (WPA), which creates jobs in many fields.

- Child-star **Shirley Temple** is named Hollywood's top box office attraction, a position she will hold for four years.

George Gershwin (on left) pens *Porgy and Bess*, a new opera, which opens in New York and runs for 124 performances. Rouben Mamoulian (on right) directs.

- President **Roosevelt is re-elected**, winning more than 60% of the popular vote.

- Margaret Mitchell's (center) Civil War novel, ***Gone with the Wind***, is an immediate best-seller. The movie is released in 1939, wins the Oscar for Best Picture, and stars Clark Gable (on left) and Vivien Leigh (on right). The heroine had originally been named Pansy, but Mitchell changes the name before publication to Scarlett O'Hara.

Clark Gable, *Gone with the Wind* author Margaret Mitchell (center), and Vivien Leigh.

- The **Baseball Hall of Fame elects** its first five honorees: Babe Ruth, Ty Cobb, Honus Wagner, Christy Mathewson, and Walter Johnson.

- **Jesse Owens, an African-American athlete**, wins four gold medals at the Olympics held in Germany. Hitler, who believes that black people are inferior to whites, is not pleased.

After five years of construction, Boulder Dam, the world's largest, is completed in the Colorado River's Black Canyon. Its name will later be changed to **Hoover Dam**.

1937

- **The Golden Gate Bridge**, spanning San Francisco Bay, opens. Its 4,200-foot middle span is the longest in the world to date.

- **Amelia Earhart**, a pioneering aviator, disappears somewhere in the Pacific during an attempt to fly around the world.

- Joe Louis, nicknamed **"The Brown Bomber,"** wins the world heavyweight boxing championship.

- American volunteers join the Republican forces in the **Spanish Civil War**. They are fighting against the Nationalists, who are supported by Hitler.

- The *Hindenburg*, a zeppelin (airship) carrying passengers from Germany to America, bursts into flames while landing in New Jersey. Thirty-five people are killed.

1938

In what is promoted as the "Match of the Century,"
the undersized racing horse **Seabiscuit** (in the lead) beats the
1–4 favorite War Admiral. Forty million Americans hear the
race over the radio.

- **Hitler's forces annex Austria**. Later in Munich, British and French officials agree to Hitler's takeover of part of Czechoslovakia.

- **Thornton Wilder's** play *Our Town* wins the Pulitzer Prize for drama.

- Chester Carlson invents **Xerography**, a process that makes it easy to copy, or "Xerox," documents.

- The character **Superman** is introduced in a comic book, *Action Comics No. 1*. Sixty-two years later a copy of that comic book will be sold to a collector for $1,000,000.

1939

- **Hollywood has a banner year**, releasing such great films as *Gone with the Wind*, *The Wizard of Oz*, *Stagecoach*, *Ninotchka*, and *Mr. Smith Goes to Washington*.

- African-American singer **Marian Anderson** is denied permission to sing at a concert hall controlled by the Daughters of the American Revolution. First Lady Eleanor Roosevelt arranges for Anderson to sing on the steps of the Lincoln Memorial instead.

- **Pan American Airlines** begins the first transatlantic passenger service, flying from New York to England and France. Passengers pay $375 for a one-way flight in the airlines' *Yankee Clipper*, which makes its landings on water.

- **World War II begins** after Hitler invades Poland on September 1, causing Great Britain and France to declare war on Germany.

At a picnic at his home in Hyde Park, New York, President Roosevelt introduces King George VI and Queen Elizabeth (his wife) of Great Britain to an American treat, hot dogs.

From left to right: Eleanor Roosevelt, King George, Sarah Roosevelt (FDR's mother), Queen Elizabeth, and President Franklin Roosevelt.

Remembering the
1940s

The first half of the 1940s was dominated by World War II. As U.S. troops fought Germany in Europe and the Japanese in the Pacific, those at home rolled up their sleeves and manned the factories, collected scrap, planted vegetable gardens, and did whatever else they could to support the war effort. More than a million U.S. troops were killed or wounded in the bloodiest conflict ever fought. And when that war ended with the unconditional surrender of Germany and Japan, the Cold War began.

But the mood at the end of the war was one of optimism. There were plenty of jobs, the economy was growing, returning G.I.s were able to get higher education and buy homes, and the future looked bright.

Americans work together in their community "Victory Gardens."

1940

Novels published this year include Richard Wright's *Native Son*, William Faulkner's *The Hamlet*, and Ernest Hemingway's *For Whom the Bell Tolls*. For children there is *Pat the Bunny*, one of the all-time best-selling children's books.

Ernest Hemingway (on left) shaking hands with Sinclair Lewis.

- President **Franklin D. Roosevelt is elected** to an unprecedented third term.

- Congress passes the **Selective Training and Service Act**, establishing the country's first peacetime draft. All men between the ages of 21 and 35 are required to register.

The average cost of a house is $6,550.
The average annual income is $1,900. A gallon of gas costs 18 cents, a loaf of bread 8 cents.

- The **Pennsylvania Turnpike opens**. It is the country's first toll superhighway.

- In January, Ida May Fuller of Rutland, Vermont, is issued the country's **first Social Security Check**, for $22.54.

1941

South Dakota's **Mount Rushmore** memorial, begun in 1927, is completed. The heads of Presidents Washington, Jefferson, Theodore Roosevelt, and Lincoln are carved out of granite rock.

- Yankee center fielder **Joe DiMaggio** hits safely in 56 consecutive games. Red Sox slugger Ted Williams bats .406 for the season. Both records still stand.

Moviegoers are treated to **two films that become classics:** the Orson Welles masterpiece *Citizen Kane*, and *The Maltese Falcon*, starring Humphrey Bogart as hard-boiled detective Sam Spade.

- On Sunday, December 7, Japanese planes launch a surprise attack on the U.S. naval base at Hawaii's Pearl Harbor. FDR calls it **"a date which will live in infamy."**

- A few hours **after striking Pearl Harbor**, the Japanese attack Wake Island. The outmanned U.S. Marine garrison there holds out for two weeks before surrendering.

- The **U.S. declares war on Japan** the day after Pearl Harbor, and on Germany three days later.

1942

At the University of Chicago, physicist **Enrico Fermi** produces the world's first controlled nuclear chain reaction— an achievement that makes the atomic bomb possible.

$$-\frac{\hbar}{i}\frac{\partial}{\partial t} = \frac{p^2}{2m} \cdot \frac{Ze^2}{r}$$

$$\alpha = \frac{\hbar^2}{ec}$$

- **With war hysteria high**, the government forces some 120,000 Japanese-American men, women, and children—most of them U.S. citizens—into internment camps.

- After **U.S. troops surrender to the Japanese** on Luzon Island in the Philippines, thousands die on the Bataan Death March, a brutal 70-mile trek to a Japanese detention camp.

- **Nationwide rationing begins**. Coupons will be issued for food, tires, clothing, gasoline, and other goods.

- Tuskegee, Alabama: The first class of African-Americans in a flight-training program graduates. Several hundred **Tuskegee Airmen** will fly with distinction with the U.S. Army Air Corps.

- The **U.S. Navy defeats the Japanese fleet** in the Battle of Midway, a turning point of the war in the Pacific. Meanwhile, American and British troops invade North Africa.

1943

The government urges Americans to **grow their own vegetables**. "Victory Gardens" spring up everywhere, producing as much as 44% of the country's vegetable crop.

The landmark musical *Oklahoma!* opens to acclaim in New York and makes box-office history, running on Broadway for five years and nine months.

- **Norman Rockwell** paints *Rosie the Riveter*, a symbol of women's new wartime role in the labor force.

- From **North Africa** the Allies move on to Sicily, then the Italian mainland. In the Pacific, beginning on Guadalcanal, naval forces slowly retake islands from the Japanese in fierce battles.

- Congress creates the **Women's Army Corps (WAC)**, one of several women's military units that play important roles in the war.

Dressed in a **bathing suit** and looking flirtatiously over her shoulder, Betty Grable poses for the photograph that makes her the number-one pinup girl of World War II.

1944

Under **General Dwight D. Eisenhower**, the Allies invade Normandy, France on D-Day, June 6.

Eisenhower (right), and talking with the troops, (below).

- Assassination attempt on **Hitler** fails.

- Congress passes the **G.I. Bill of Rights**, which will enable millions of servicemen to go to school and buy homes or farms after the war.

- Despite declining health, **President Roosevelt wins a fourth** term, defeating Thomas Dewey.

- The **best-selling novel of the 1940s** is Kathleen Winsor's bodice-ripper *Forever Amber*. Despite being banned in 14 states, it sells 100,000 copies its first week.

Seventeen **magazine** begins publication. Aimed at teenage girls, its first issue sells 400,000 copies in six days.

1945

Scientists explode the first **atomic bomb** in the New Mexico desert, ushering in the nuclear age. A month later, atomic bombs are dropped on Hiroshima and Nagasaki, Japan.

- Shortly after being re-elected, the country mourns the **sudden death of President Franklin D. Roosevelt**, at age 63, from a cerebral hemorrhage. Harry Truman is sworn in as president.

- Allied troops are stunned by the discovery of **Nazi death camps at Auschwitz**, Buchenwald, and many other places.

- **World War II ends** when Germany surrenders in May. Japan surrenders in August.

Life **magazine** publishes one of its most famous photographs: Alfred Eisenstaedt's shot of an exuberant sailor kissing a white-clad nurse in New York's Times Square, in celebration of the war's end.

1946

- Winston Churchill warns of Communist expansion in his **"Iron Curtain" speech** at Westminster College in Fulton, Missouri. The speech marks the beginning of the Cold War.

- **Earl Tupper**, a DuPont chemist, develops Tupperware from polyethylene, a new plastic. A few years later, the Tupperware home party is born.

The great athlete
Babe Didrikson Zaharias begins her streak of winning 17 amateur golf tournaments in a row.

- **Painter Georgia O'Keeffe** is the first woman artist to have a retrospective at New York's Museum of Modern Art.

- **Dr. Benjamin Spock** publishes *Dr. Spock's Baby and Child Care: A Handbook for Parents of Developing Children from Birth Through Adolescence.* The book sells for 25 cents and becomes the bible of childrearing.

- In what becomes the first year of the postwar **Baby Boom**, new births skyrocket as returning G.I.s start families.

1947

- To meet the need of returning veterans for affordable housing, **builder William Levitt** begins the first Levittown, a planned community of thousands of mass-produced houses on Long Island, New York.

- The Reynolds Metals company creates **Reynolds Wrap Aluminum Foil**, which transforms the way food is cooked and stored.

- **Jackie Robinson breaks major-league baseball's color barrier** when, at Branch Rickey's invitation, he joins the Brooklyn Dodgers. He becomes National League Rookie of the Year for 1947.

- **Marlon Brando triumphs** as Stanley Kowalski in Tennessee Williams's Pulitzer Prize-winning play *A Streetcar Named Desire*. The opening-night Broadway audience applauds for half an hour.

- Full-scale commercial television broadcasting begins, and **Americans start to buy sets for their homes**. Howdy Doody and Milton Berle are TV's first big stars.

Designer **Christian Dior** unveils "The New Look," featuring fitted jackets, nipped-in waists, and full calf-length skirts. It is a sharp contrast to the styles of the war years.

1948

- New to the marketplace are Edwin Herbert Land's revolutionary **Polaroid camera**, and **Scrabble**, a game that takes a few years to catch on.

- In an **escalation of the Cold War**, the Soviet Union blockades Berlin. The U.S. and Britain airlift supplies to the city and eventually break the blockade.

- TV news anchor **John Cameron Swayze**, host of NBC's nightly news show "Camel News Caravan," is required by the sponsor to have a lighted cigarette in view at all times.

- **NASCAR**—the National Association of Stock Car Auto Racing—sponsors its first race at Daytona Beach, Florida.

- President Truman issues an executive order **ending segregation** in the armed forces and the civil service.

In one of the **great political upsets in American history**, Harry S. Truman defeats Thomas E. Dewey and is elected President.

1949

Arthur Miller's Pulitzer Prize-winning play *The Death of a Salesman* is the first play to become a Book-of-the-Month Club selection.

- **"The Goldbergs,"** an enormously popular radio series, moves to television, where it becomes TV's first hit situation comedy.

- **President Truman** proposes compulsory health insurance for all Americans. Opponents, including the American Medical Association, label the idea socialism.

- **Cortisone is discovered**, giving doctors a new tool to fight rheumatoid arthritis.

Popular songs include "Mule Train," " 'A' You're Adorable," "Some Enchanted Evening" (from the hit musical *South Pacific*), and **"Rudolph the Red-Nosed Reindeer."**

Remembering the **1950s**

Just five years after the end of World War II, America found itself at war again, this time in Korea. This "police action" to contain Communism was followed by more years of international Cold War tension. At home, the country experienced McCarthyism, a brutal witch-hunt for American communists. Later, the struggle to end segregation of the races in schools and on public transportation dominated the headlines.

But although the 1950s were not years of tranquillity, there were great accomplishments to be proud of: medical advances like the polio vaccine and organ transplants, and technological breakthroughs like jet planes, computers, and space satellites. And of course there was time for entertainment and fun—hula hoops and 3-D movies, rock 'n' roll and "I Love Lucy," Elvis Presley, and Marilyn Monroe.

1950

North Korean troops invade South Korea. U.S. troops, with United Nations backing, come to the aid of the South Koreans, while China aids the North.

Senator **Joseph McCarthy** of Wisconsin leads a campaign to expose alleged Communists and their sympathizers in government, television, and movies. Many innocent people lose their jobs and reputations.

- The first national **Emmys** are awarded: Milton Berle and his weekly television show, "The Texaco Star Theater," are the big winners.

- The **minimum wage is now 75 cents** an hour, and the median family income is $3,210. Gas costs 18 cents a gallon, and the price of a black-and-white television set is $250.

- **The Diners Club** introduces a cardboard credit card. American Express will not issue its first credit card until 1958, and plastic cards will not appear until 1959.

1951

The **first computer** for use in business, UNIVAC 1, is produced by the Eckert-Mauchly Computer Company and Remington Rand for the U.S. Census Bureau. It weighs 29,000 pounds.

- "I Love Lucy," a half-hour television comedy with **Lucille Ball and Desi Arnaz**, debuts. It will continue for six years and remain popular in reruns.

- **Bobby Thomson's** ninth-inning three-run homer wins the National League pennant for the New York Giants, who beat their archrivals, the Brooklyn Dodgers.

- **President Truman replaces General Douglas MacArthur**, leader of U.S. troops in the Korean War, because he openly disagrees with Truman's policies. MacArthur tells Congress that "old soldiers never die, they just fade away."

The world's first **power-generating nuclear plant** is opened near Arco, Idaho.

- **The first hydrogen bomb** is tested by the U.S. on Eniwetok in the Marshall Islands, about 3,000 miles west of Hawaii.

Elizabeth II becomes Queen of England upon the death of her father, King George VI.

- *Bwana Devil* and other **3-D movies** attract large audiences, who don't mind wearing the necessary glasses.

- The new ocean liner **SS *United States*** sails from New York to England in a record-breaking 3 days, 10 hours, and 40 minutes. Its average speed is just shy of 40 miles per hour.

- **General Dwight D. Eisenhower** defeats Adlai Stevenson in the presidential election. As he had promised, Eisenhower goes to Korea to help end the war there.

Rocky Marciano knocks out Jersey Joe Walcott to take the heavyweight boxing crown.

1953

Dr. Jonas Salk reveals that he has produced a vaccine that prevents polio.

- **Julius and Ethel Rosenberg** are executed for passing military secrets to the Soviet Union. They are the first (and only) U.S. citizens to be sentenced to death for espionage.

- The Chevrolet Corvette, a **sports car with a convertible roof**, is introduced. The first models all have white bodies and red interiors.

- Among this year's **notable movies** are *From Here to Eternity*, *Shane*, *Gentlemen Prefer Blondes* starring Marilyn Monroe, and *The Robe*, the first film to use the new wide-screen CinemaScope format.

- The first **color television sets** go on sale for $1,175.

1954

- Senator **Joseph McCarthy's** hearings into alleged communism in the U.S. Army keep Americans glued to their TV sets. Later, he is officially censured by his fellow Senators for abusing his legislative powers.

- A medical milestone this year is the **first organ transplant**: A kidney is taken from one twin and given to his brother.

- **Popular songs** this year include "Mr. Sandman," "Hey There," "Secret Love," "Young at Heart," and the rock 'n' roll hit "Rock Around the Clock," by Bill Haley and the Comets.

- **Roger Bannister**, a British medical student, becomes the first person to run a mile in less than four minutes. His time is 3 minutes, 59.4 seconds.

- The words **"under God"** are officially added to the Pledge of Allegiance by President Eisenhower.

Joseph McCarthy (left),talking with Roy Cohn, Chief Counsel of Senate Investigations Subcommittee.

In a landmark case, **_Brown vs. Board of Education_** of Topeka, Kansas, the Supreme Court rules that American public schools may not segregate students by race.

Pictured from left to right, lawyers George E.C. Hayes, Thurgood Marshall, and James M. Nabrit.

1955

- **Rosa Parks**, an African-American woman, is arrested in Montgomery, Alabama, because she refuses to move to the "colored section" at the back of the bus. This leads to a boycott of the bus system led by Martin Luther King, Jr.

- The new **U.S. Air Force Academy** welcomes its first class at temporary headquarters near Denver. Its permanent home at Colorado Springs won't be ready until 1958.

- A series of **Walt Disney television shows** about Davy Crockett, the western frontiersman, sets off a Crockett craze around the country. Kids sing "The Ballad of Davy Crockett" and buy Crockett toys, shirts, and above all, coonskin hats.

- Actor **James Dean**, star of the new movies *Rebel Without a Cause* and *East of Eden*, dies in an automobile crash at the age of 24.

- The **first McDonald's franchise** restaurant opens in Des Plaines, Illinois.

1956

Elvis Presley records five number-one singles this year: "Heartbreak Hotel," "Don't Be Cruel," "Hound Dog," "Love Me Tender," and "I Want You, I Need You, I Love You."

- The **Italian ocean liner *Andrea Doria*** collides with another ship and sinks off the coast of New England. Most of the 1,700 passengers and the crew are rescued, but 46 people die.

- American artist **Jackson Pollock**, whose paintings were made by dripping or pouring paint on canvas, dies in an auto accident. Widely derided by many people, his abstract expressionist paintings will one day sell for millions of dollars.

- **Pitcher Don Larsen** of the New York Yankees throws the first perfect game in World Series history.

- The **Dow Jones Industrial Average** hits 500 for the first time.

American film star **Grace Kelly** marries Prince Rainier of Monaco in what is called "The Wedding of the Century."

1957

The new musicals **West Side Story** (above, in rehearsal, center is Chita Rivera, second from left is choreographer Jerome Robbins) and *The Music Man* draw huge audiences on Broadway.

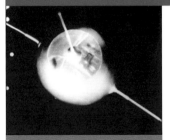

The Soviet Union launches the first man-made space satellite, known as **Sputnik**, starting the space race with the U.S.

- To the dismay of their fans, the **Brooklyn Dodgers** and New York Giants move to California.

- The **U.S. Surgeon General** announces the results of a study that shows there is a direct link between smoking cigarettes and lung cancer.

- **President Eisenhower sends troops to Little Rock**, Arkansas, to assure the safety of nine African-American children attending a previously all-white high school.

- The **Mackinac Bridge** opens in Michigan, and becomes the world's longest suspension bridge to date.

1958

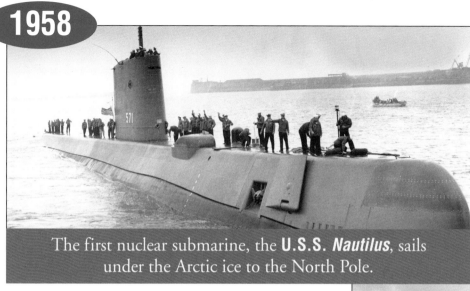

The first nuclear submarine, the **U.S.S. *Nautilus***, sails under the Arctic ice to the North Pole.

- **Ford introduces a new line of cars**, the Edsel. It is a resounding flop. With much better results, Toyota sells its first cars in the U.S.

- National Airlines offers the **first jet passenger service** in the U.S. The first transatlantic jet passenger service is inaugurated by BOAC.

- President Eisenhower sends U.S. marines to Lebanon to support that country's shaky government.

The craze for **hula hoops** sweeps the country. Twenty million of the plastic hoops are sold in six months.

1959

A 32-year-old Fidel Castro takes power in Cuba.

- The **first Grammy Awards** are handed out, with Ella Fitzgerald and Perry Como named as best vocalists.

- Queen Elizabeth II and President Eisenhower officially open the **Saint Lawrence Seaway**, which allows large ships to sail from the Atlantic Ocean to the Great Lakes.

- **Alaska** and **Hawaii** become the 49th and 50th states.

- Ruth Handler creates the **Barbie Doll**, which she names after her daughter.

Dwight D. Eisenhower showing off the restyled American flag, which includes stars for the two added states.

Remembering the **1960s**

The 1960s were years of turmoil and change. A president, his brother, and a revered civil rights leader were all assassinated. The country was torn apart by an unpopular war in Vietnam, and violence dogged the civil-rights movement. But there were also monumental achievements, including landmark civil rights legislation and the landing of the first human on the moon.

Socially, the decade witnessed the onset of a new feminist revolution and the birth of the hippie movement. Young people rejected the values of their parents' generation and embraced a new lifestyle. Fashion reflected the shifts, with Jacqueline Kennedy's suits and pillbox hats giving way to unisex bell-bottom jeans and tie-dyed shirts. By the end of the decade, changes had been set in motion that would determine the character and the direction of the country for decades to come.

1960

- *The Fantasticks* opens off-Broadway in New York City. It will run for an amazing 42 years, until 2002.

- **Hugh Hefner** opens the first Playboy Club in Chicago, featuring scantily clad cocktail waitresses called Playboy Bunnies.

- A **U.S. U-2 spy plane** is shot down inside the Soviet Union. The pilot, Francis Gary Powers, is imprisoned, then traded for a Soviet spy. The incident heightens Cold War tensions.

- In a milestone for meteorology, **NASA launches TIROS-1**, the first successful weather satellite. In another scientific milestone, physicist Theodore Maiman builds the first workable laser.

- **John F. Kennedy defeats Richard M. Nixon** in one of the closest Presidential elections in U.S. history. Kennedy becomes the country's youngest president, and its first Catholic chief executive.

Gregory Peck, with Mary Badham, who plays his daughter Scout.

One of this year's novels includes ***To Kill a Mockingbird***, Harper Lee's Pulitzer Prize-winning story about racial injustice. It will be made into a hit movie starring Gregory Peck.

1961

- **President Kennedy**—whose inaugural address includes the challenge, "Ask not what your country can do for you—ask what you can do for your country"—establishes the Peace Corps, which sends volunteers to work in underdeveloped countries.

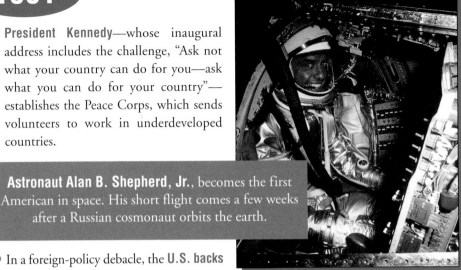

Astronaut Alan B. Shepherd, Jr., becomes the first American in space. His short flight comes a few weeks after a Russian cosmonaut orbits the earth.

- In a foreign-policy debacle, the **U.S. backs an attempt by anti-Cuban** exiles to invade Cuba and overthrow Fidel Castro. The invasion, at the Bay of Pigs, is a total failure.

- **Yankee Roger Maris hits 61 home runs**, breaking Babe Ruth's 1927 record, one few thought could be broken.

- The **federal minimum wage is set at $1.15** an hour, rising to $1.25 in two years. Coverage is expanded to include 3,600,000 new workers.

- New York's **Metropolitan Museum of Art** pays a record $2,300,000 for Rembrandt's painting *Aristotle Contemplating the Bust of Homer*.

1962

First Lady Jacqueline Kennedy conducts a televised tour of the White House. It is watched by some 56 million viewers.

- Following the discovery of **Soviet missiles in Cuba**, the U.S. blockades the island. After a frightening week, during which nuclear war is threatened, Russia agrees to remove its missiles.

- Philadelphia Warriors basketball star **Wilt Chamberlain sets a record by scoring 100 points** in a game against the New York Knicks.

- **Riots break out at the University of Mississippi** when an African-American, James Meredith, tries to enroll. President Kennedy sends Federal troops to protect Meredith.

- **Rachel Carson's book** *Silent Spring*, a study of the damaging effects of DDT and other pesticides, helps launch the environmental movement.

- The Supreme Court rules that any **prayer in public schools** is unconstitutional.

1963

From the steps of the Washington, DC Lincoln Memorial, **Dr. Martin Luther King, Jr.** delivers his unforgettable "I Have a Dream" speech to a crowd of 250,000 civil-rights demonstrators.

- **The Beatles** release their first album, "Please Please Me" in the U.K.

- During the filming of the multimillion-dollar epic *Cleopatra*, **Elizabeth Taylor** and co-star Richard Burton engage in a scandalous affair.

- Civil rights leader **Medgar Evers is killed** outside his home in Jackson, Mississippi.

- Betty Friedan writes *The Feminine Mystique*, a book that questions the role of modern suburban housewives. It sparks the **feminist revolution**.

The country is stunned by the **assassination of President Kennedy** in Dallas, Texas, in November. With Jacqueline Kennedy at his side aboard Air Force One, Lyndon Johnson is sworn in as President.

Jackie Kennedy with her children, Ted Kennedy, (left), and Robert Kennedy (right), at the President's funeral.

1964

The Beatles make their U.S. debut on *The Ed Sullivan Show*. The country comes to a standstill as 73 million people watch.

- **Cassius Clay** defeats heavyweight champion Sonny Liston. Clay will convert to Islam, change his name to Muhammad Ali, and in 1967 refuse to serve in Vietnam.

- Elected president by an overwhelming majority, **Lyndon Johnson** pushes a landmark civil rights bill through Congress. It strikes down segregation in public places and in education.

- *Hello, Dolly!* is the musical-comedy hit of the season, and Louis Armstrong's recording of the show's title song sells over a million copies.

- A black Mississippian and two white New Yorkers—**volunteers registering black voters**—are murdered outside Philadelphia, Mississippi.

The Barbie doll for girls inspires Hasbro to design **G.I. Joe**, an action figure-with-wardrobe for boys. The doll is a huge success.

1965

U.S. combat forces are sent to **South Vietnam**, and U.S. fighter pilots carry out the first bombing raid of the war. Protest demonstrations take place across the U.S.

- The **biggest blackout in U.S. history** hits the northeastern United States and Canada. Thirty million people are without power for as long as 13 hours.

- Congress passes many of President Johnson's Great Society programs, including **Medicare**, an antipoverty bill, and a voting-rights bill. Head Start is launched.

- Los Angeles Dodgers **pitcher Sandy Koufax** pitches a perfect game—the fourth no-hit game of his career.

- **Dr. Martin Luther King, Jr.**, leads a five-day civil rights march from Selma to Montgomery, Alabama.

A monument to pioneers, St. Louis's steel **Gateway Arch**, designed by Eero Saarinen, is completed.

1966

- As U.S. involvement in **Vietnam** escalates, antiwar protests grow.

- In its so-called **Miranda decision**, the Supreme Court rules that suspects must be informed of their rights before they can be questioned.

- "**Star Trek**" has its television premier. Canceled after three years, the franchise goes on to become an international phenomenon, with followers called "Trekkies" attending Star Trek conventions.

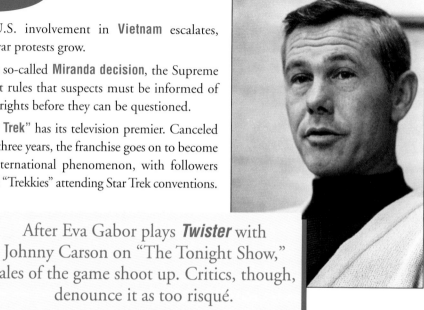

After Eva Gabor plays *Twister* with Johnny Carson on "The Tonight Show," sales of the game shoot up. Critics, though, denounce it as too risqué.

- Martin Luther King, Jr.'s **non-violent strategy** is challenged by young militants such as Stokely Carmichael, a proponent of black power.

NBC, the National Broadcasting Company, becomes **the first television network** to produce all of its new TV programs in color.

1967

- **Astronauts** Edward White, Virgil Grissom, and Roger Chaffee are killed in a fire in their space capsule while it sits on its launching pad.

- **The first Super Bowl is played in Los Angeles.** The Green Bay Packers defeat the Kansas City Chiefs, 35–10.

- The **first microwave** model for home use makes its appearance.

- More than 100,000 young hippies flock to San Francisco's Haight-Ashbury neighborhood for the **Summer of Love**—a counterculture celebration marked by music, drugs, and free love.

- Elsewhere, the summer is marked by violence as **race riots** rip through U.S. cities. They are particularly destructive in Newark, NJ, and Detroit, MI.

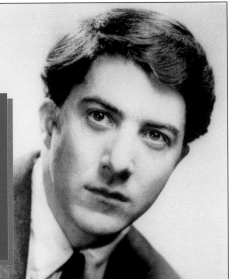

The Graduate, starring Dustin Hoffman and Anne Bancroft, captures a young generation's discontent with their parents' values and lifestyles.

1968

Robert F. Kennedy.

- The country is stunned by **two assassinations:** Senator Robert F. Kennedy is killed while campaigning for the Democratic presidential nomination. Dr. Martin Luther King, Jr., is shot on a hotel balcony in Memphis.

- **U.S. involvement in the Vietnam War reaches its peak.** North Vietnam launches the deadly Tet offensive. Antiwar protests escalate. Police attack protesters outside the Democratic convention in Chicago.

- **Done in by the unpopular war,** President Johnson announces he will not run again. Richard Nixon—who promises to end U.S. involvement in Vietnam—defeats Hubert Humphrey.

- *Hair: The American Tribal Love-Rock Musical* opens on Broadway. Its tale of life in the **"Age of Aquarius"** features rock music, anti-establishment themes, and some nudity.

- **"60 Minutes"** begins its long television run. The popular program introduces a new way of reporting the news.

- **Dr. Denton Cooley** performs the first successful heart transplant in the United States, a few months after South African surgeon Christian Bernard pioneered the operation.

Christian Bernard (center), with two other doctors.

1969

A tumultuous decade is capped by a momentous achievement: **Astronaut Neil Armstrong** becomes the first human to walk on the moon. Armstrong says, "That's one small step for [a] man, one giant leap for mankind." Pictured at right is Edwin "Buzz" Aldrin who was with Armstrong on the historic mission.

- **"Sesame Street"** is launched, with the goal of educating preschool children. The song "Rubber Duckie" becomes a hit.

- The U.S. Department of Agriculture **bans the use of the pesticide DDT** in homes and gardens. DDT will be completely banned in 1972.

- Parker Brothers introduces the **Nerf Ball**. More than four million are sold by year's end.

In the counterculture event of the 1960s, more than 400,000 flower children flock to a farm near **Woodstock, NY,** for "3 days of peace and music." Among the entertainers are Richie Havens, the Grateful Dead, Janis Joplin, the Who, Jefferson Airplane, and Jimi Hendrix.

Remembering the **1970s**

Americans didn't have a lot to be happy about in the 1970s. The intervention in Vietnam and the deep divisions at home caused by the war, along with Watergate and Nixon's resignation from the presidency, shook the nation's confidence in its government and its military. An Arab oil embargo and a nuclear plant scare in Pennsylvania underlined the seriousness of the country's energy problem. And at decade's end, when Iran held Americans hostage in Tehran, many Americans felt angry and powerless.

Still, when the country celebrated its bicentennial in 1976, the year-long festivities were marked by a swell of patriotism. Americans looked back proudly at their nation's enormous accomplishments: Creating a transcontinental world power from 13 colonies clustered along the Atlantic seaboard; making countless breakthroughs in medicine, science, and technology; and fulfilling to a large degree the founders' dreams of freedom and democracy.

1970

The year's most popular movie is *Love Story*, with its oft-repeated line, "Love means never having to say you're sorry."

- **The war in Vietnam spreads** into Cambodia, where the North Vietnamese store weapons and supplies. At home, opposition to the war escalates. Four unarmed students are killed by the National Guard during anti-war protests at Kent State University in Ohio, and two students were slain by police at Jackson State College in Florida.

- **It's a sad year for rock fans.** The Beatles break up, and Janis Joplin and Jimi Hendrix both die at the age of 27.

- **The north tower of the World Trade Center opens** in New York City. It becomes the tallest building in the world to date. The south tower will open in 1972.

Congress **votes to ban cigarette advertising** on television and radio.

1971

"All in the Family" debuts on television; it uses the bigotry of its lead character, Archie Bunker, as a source of comedy.

- Daniel Ellsberg, an analyst at the Rand Corporation, releases to the press the so-called **Pentagon Papers**, thousands of top-secret documents revealing that U.S. military leaders do not believe the war in Vietnam is winnable. Opposition to the war increases.

- **The 26th amendment**, lowering the voting age from 21 to 18, is ratified.

- Tennis star **Billie Jean King** is the first woman athlete to earn more than $100,000 in a single season of competition.

The first phase of **Walt Disney World**, including the Magic Kingdom, opens in Orlando, Florida.

1972

- **President Nixon visits China,** opening a new era in U.S.–Chinese relations.

- For the first time, women are among the new group of FBI agent graduates.

California swimmer Mark Spitz wins seven gold medals at the Olympic Games in Munich, Germany.

- *The Godfather*, the first of three movies about an Italian-American gangster family, is a huge hit. It will win Oscars as Best Picture and for Marlon Brando as Best Actor.

- Five men are caught breaking into Democratic headquarters in Washington's **Watergate Hotel**. The full story of the break-in will not be known for another year.

- **President Nixon wins** re-election, easily beating Senator George McGovern.

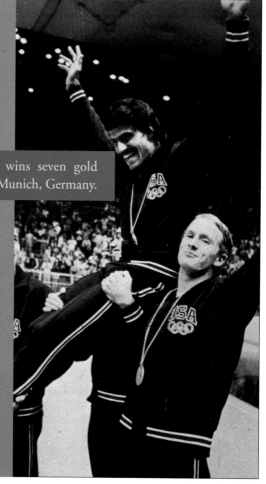

Investigations into the **Watergate break-in** show that President Nixon's closest advisers were involved in an attempted cover-up of the crime. Senate hearings attempt to reveal the extent of the president's involvement.

Pictured in happier times, First Lady Pat Nixon, President Richard Nixon, and Vice President, Spiro Agnew.

- **U.S. troops** are withdrawn from Vietnam.

- In a controversial decision, the **Supreme Court rules** that a woman's right to privacy includes the right to have an abortion.

- **Vice President Spiro Agnew resigns** after being charged with extortion, bribery, and income tax evasion. Congressman Gerald Ford is appointed Vice President.

- Because the U.S. supports Israel when it is attacked by Arab nations, the **Arabs cease shipments of oil to the U.S.** Gasoline is in short supply. There are long lines at gas stations, and rationing measures are introduced.

- Among the year's technological achievements are the **Sears Tower in Chicago**, which now becomes the world's tallest building to date, and Skylab, NASA's orbiting space station.

Patty Hearst, a 19-year-old San Francisco heiress, is kidnapped by a revolutionary group called the Symbionese National Liberation Army. Later she is seen assisting her captors in a bank robbery and is jailed despite claims she was brainwashed.

- In baseball **Hank Aaron** hits his 715th career home run, breaking Babe Ruth's record. Aaron will hit 40 more before he retires.

- Writer **Stephen King** publishes his first horror novel, *Carrie*. In future years, more than 350 million of King's books will be sold.

- The year's strangest fad is **streaking**—running naked through public places. One such incident occurs at this year's Academy Awards ceremony.

- **President Nixon's participation** in the effort to obstruct justice in the Watergate affair is no longer in doubt. To avoid being removed from office by Congress, he resigns, the first president ever to do so. Vice President Gerald Ford becomes President.

1975

The last U.S. citizens remaining in Saigon, along with Vietnamese refugees who had helped the U.S., are evacuated by helicopter from rooftops and flown to safety on offshore aircraft carriers. The city soon falls to the North Vietnamese (pictured) forces.

- **Elizabeth Ann Seton**, founder of the American Sisters of Charity, is the first U.S.–born person to be canonized by the Catholic Church.

- Despite opposition by the Defense Department, **Congress votes to allow women** to attend the nation's military academies.

- **The Louisiana Superdome** opens in New Orleans. It is the biggest fixed dome in the world, with a diameter of 680 feet. The stadium can hold over 85,000 people.

- Among **this year's new television programs** are NBC's "Saturday Night Live" and "Wheel of Fortune" and ABC's "Good Morning America."

1976

- The **United States celebrates its Bicentennial**, the two hundredth anniversary of the Declaration of Independence. Shown above is a Bicentennial Wagon Train as it crosses the Allegheny River in Pittsburgh, PA.

- **President Ford defeats Ronald Reagan** in a fight for the Republican presidential nomination, but loses to Democrat Jimmy Carter in the November election.

- For the first time, **a group of baseball players become free agents** when their contracts expire. Previously, players belonged to one club for life and had to accept whatever salary that club offered. Soon free agency spreads to other sports.

- "Happy Days," "Laverne and Shirley," and "M*A*S*H" are among the **top-rated television shows**, and *Rocky* is the year's most popular movie.

Novelist Saul Bellow wins the Nobel Prize for literature.

1977

- The **personal computer era** takes a giant leap forward with the introduction of the easy-to-use Apple II. The cost is $1,298 for 4K RAM.
- **Congress passes legislation** that will raise the minimum wage in stages from the current $2.30 an hour to $3.35 an hour by 1981.
- President Carter signs the **Panama Canal Treaties** which give Panama control over the canal in a step-by-step process ending in 1999.
- Americans are enthralled by the television miniseries **"Roots,"** which traces the history of an African-American family.

The movie *Saturday Night Fever* and its sound track featuring the Bee Gees set off a disco dance craze. Also this year, the science fiction epic *Star Wars* becomes the highest-grossing movie in film history.

1978

- **David Thompson,** a player for basketball's Denver Nuggets, signs a contract that will pay him $800,000 a year for five years. This is the most money ever paid an athlete in team sports to date.

- **Four hundred members of a cult** led by Jim Jones commit mass suicide in Guyana, South America.

- Public field trials of a **cellular mobile phone system** are begun in Chicago by Illinois Bell.

- **Pope John Paul I dies** just 33 days after assuming the papacy. The new pope is John Paul II.

- *Space Invaders,* an arcade video game, becomes an instant hit worldwide. Two years later, a home version for video consoles will be introduced by Atari.

At **Camp David** in Maryland, President Carter (center) brokers an agreement between Menachem Begin (right) of Israel and Anwar el-Sadat (left) of Egypt that will lead to a peace treaty between the two nations.

1979

- Sony introduces the **Walkman**, a portable audio cassette player. The cost is about $100.

- In March, an **Islamic Republic led by Ayatollah Khomeini** is established in Iran. In November, Iranian students seize the American embassy in Tehran and hold 66 people, mostly Americans, as hostages there.

- A malfunction at the **Three Mile Island nuclear power plant** in Pennsylvania results in the release of a small amount of radioactive gas. Fearful of a meltdown, some 140,000 leave their homes, but technicians are able to get the problem under control.

- The **average yearly income has risen** to $ 17,500. The average cost of a house is now $58,100.

Michael Jackson (center) releases his first solo album, *Off the Wall*. It has sold more than 20 million copies worldwide.

Remembering the **1980s**

The 1980s saw a resurgence of conservatism in the U.S., as Americans put the turmoil of the 1970s behind them and elected a conservative Republican as their president. Ronald Reagan worked to reduce the role of government at home and fight the spread of Communism abroad. By the end of his second term, he had the highest approval rating of any president since Franklin Roosevelt.

Average incomes rose during the decade, from $19,170 in 1980 to $27,210 in 1989. At the same time, the cost of most things increased significantly. In 1980 a new house cost $68,714; by 1989 the cost was $120,000. A new car that cost on average $7,210 in 1980 was $15,400 by 1989. But a gallon of gas cost less—from $1.19 in 1980 to 97 cents in 1989.

President Ronald Reagan and his wife, Nancy, wave during his inaugural parade.

1980

Mount St. Helens, a volcano in Washington State's Cascade Range, erupts. The spectacular explosion kills 57 people and does more than $1 billion of damage.

- **Republican Ronald Reagan** overwhelms President Jimmy Carter in this year's presidential election. (Carter's failure to secure the release of 52 Americans being held hostage in Iran contributes to his defeat.)

- Former Beatles member **John Lennon is killed** outside his apartment building in New York City by a deranged fan.

- In the **1980 Winter Olympics at Lake Placid, NY,** the underdog U.S. hockey team is the Cinderella gold medal winner, beating Finland after defeating a heavily favored Soviet team.

- 3M begins selling **Post-It Notes** nationwide.

Millions of viewers tune in to **"Dallas,"** a soap on TV to find out who shot J.R. Ewing, the lead character.

1981

- **MTV (Music Television),** a cable station devoted to music videos, launches with the words, "Ladies and gentlemen, rock and roll."

Sandra Day O'Connor becomes the first woman appointed to the Supreme Court.

- **IBM** introduces the personal computer. The lowest-priced IBM PC sells for $1,565— the equivalent of nearly $4,000 today.

- **The space shuttle** *Columbia*, the first reusable spaceship, voyages into orbit. A fleet of space shuttles will go on to fly hundreds of missions.

President Reagan is shot by John Hinckley, Jr., who is later committed to a mental institution. Reagan, who soon recovers, jokes that he "forgot to duck." Also hit is press secretary James Brady, who is partially paralyzed.

1982

- Steven Spielberg's movie *E.T.: The Extra-Terrestrial* is a box-office smash.

The Weather Channel goes on the air with 24-hour weather and weather-related stories.

- The Supreme Court rules that **children of illegal immigrants** have the right to public school education.
- The **NCAA** (National Collegiate Athletic Association) holds its first college basketball championship for women.

The Vietnam Veterans Memorial, designed by Maya Ying Lin, is dedicated in Washington, DC. It includes the names of the 58,267 Americans lost in the war.

1983

A new craze begins with the mass marketing of **Cabbage Patch Kids**. Demand outpaces supply, and shoppers fight one another for one of the coveted dolls.

- **In Lebanon**, 241 U.S. Marines—part of a multinational force trying to end Lebanon's bloody civil war—are killed in their barracks by a suicide bomber.

- **U.S. forces invade Grenada**, a tiny island in the Caribbean. President Reagan says the island, whose leaders have close ties to the Soviet Union and Cuba, is a Communist threat.

- The first **compact discs** are introduced in the U.S.

- Congress passes legislation designating the **third Monday in January as a federal holiday** honoring Dr. Martin Luther King, Jr.

About 106 million viewers watch the **final episode of "M*A*S*H"**—a record for a nonsports TV program.

1984

Ronald Reagan is reelected in a landslide over Walter Mondale. Mondale's running mate, Geraldine Ferraro, is the first woman nominated for vice president by a major political party.

- **Steven Spielberg and George Lucas** keep shattering box-office records, this year with the film *Indiana Jones and the Temple of Doom*.
- Disneyland in California celebrates **Donald Duck's 50th birthday** with a parade.
- Runner Carl Lewis, gymnast Mary Lou Retton, marathoner Joan Benoit, and diver Greg Louganis star in the **1984 Summer Olympics** in Los Angeles. The Soviet Union boycotts the Games.
- **After a lapse of 117 years**, the U.S. restores full diplomatic relations with the Vatican.

"The Cosby Show" begins a long run as one of TV's most popular shows. It is the first series to feature a successful, upper-middle-class African-American family.

1985

Bob Dylan (left), and Keith Richards of The Rolling Stones in Philadelphia.

Live Aid concerts are held simultaneously in London and Philadelphia to raise money for Ethiopian famine relief. An estimated 1.5 billion viewers watch worldwide. Many popular stars contribute free performances.

- **Palestinian terrorists hijack** the Italian liner *Achille Lauro* in the Mediterranean. They kill a 69-year-old wheelchair-bound American, Leon Klinghoffer, and throw his body overboard.

- In a banner year for baseball, **Nolan Ryan** becomes the first pitcher to strike out 4,000 batters, Tom Seaver and Phil Niekro become the 17th and 18th 300-game winners, and Pete Rose breaks Ty Cobb's record of 4,191 career hits.

- **The Coca-Cola Company changes the formula for Coke.** The public outcry is so great that the company quickly restores the old Coke formula under a new name, Coca-Cola Classic.

- A U.S.–French team finds the **wreck of the *Titanic*** off Newfoundland.

Matinee idol **Rock Hudson** is the first major U.S. celebrity to die of AIDS.

1986

As millions of horrified viewers watch on television, the space shuttle *Challenger* explodes seconds after its launch. Among the seven people killed is Sharon Christa McAuliffe, a teacher from New Hampshire.

- **"The Oprah Winfrey Show"** goes on air for the first time. It will run until 2011 and become U.S. television's highest-rated talk show.

- Rupert Murdoch creates **Fox Broadcasting Company** to compete with ABC, CBS, and NBC. Its first series is "The Late Show Starring Joan Rivers."

- **The Iran-Contra Affair**—a series of covert activities involving the illegal sale of U.S. arms to Iran and the funneling of funds from the sale to anti-Communist Contra insurgents in Nicaragua—embroils the Reagan administration.

- In sports, **20-year-old Mike Tyson** becomes heavyweight boxing's youngest champion ever, and Willie Shoemaker at 54, is the oldest jockey to win the Kentucky Derby.

President Reagan and Soviet leader Mikhail Gorbachev sign a historic **missile reduction treaty**, reducing the sizes of their nuclear arsenals.

- In fashion, **the miniskirt is back**, as designers in New York, London, Milan, and Paris all shorten their hemlines.

- The Supreme Court rules that **women must be admitted** to Rotary Clubs.

- The **antidepressant Prozac** is released for sale in the U.S. Within a few years annual sales will reach $1 billion.

- A five-year bull market ends when the **U.S. stock market crashes on October 19**, losing 22.6% of its value in a single day. Within two years, however, the market fully recovers.

1988

Broadway sets a box-office record, thanks to blockbuster musicals such as *The Phantom of the Opera* (pictured) and *Les Misérables*.

- Forest fires burn more than a third of **Yellowstone National Park**. More than 25,000 fire fighters from around the country fight the blazes.

- A **bomb explodes** on a Pan Am flight from London to New York as it flies over Lockerbie, Scotland. All 259 passengers, including 179 Americans, are killed.

- **The year's top movies** include *Die Hard*, the first of a hit series starring Bruce Willis, and *Rain Man*, whose star Dustin Hoffman wins an Oscar for Best Actor.

Vice President George H. W. Bush is elected President.

He pledges, "Read my lips: No new taxes"—a promise that backfires a few years later when he is forced to raise taxes.

The oil tanker ***Exxon Valdez*** runs aground off the coast of Alaska and spills millions of gallons of crude oil. The spill kills or injures hundreds of thousands of birds and animals.

- **L. Douglas Wilder is elected** governor of Virginia, becoming the country's first elected African-American governor.

- **U.S. troops invade Panama** to protect the Panama Canal, overthrow dictator Manuel Noriega, and restore democracy. Noriega is arrested and eventually convicted and imprisoned for drug trafficking and racketeering.

- **Tina Turner** wins her fifth Grammy for Best Female Rock Vocal Performance, for *Tina Live in Europe*.

- In a game against the Edmonton Oilers, Los Angeles King **Wayne Gretzky** scores his 1851st point and becomes the highest scorer in NHL history.

Remembering the **1990s**

There were many shocking headlines in U.S. newspapers in the 1990s. "O.J. SIMPSON ARRESTED FOR WIFE'S MURDER." "BOMB KILLS 168 IN OKLAHOMA CITY." "PRESIDENT CLINTON IMPEACHED." "MASSACRE AT COLUMBINE HIGH SCHOOL." "PRINCESS DIANA KILLED." These and other stories dominated the news for weeks on end.

Thankfully there was plenty to cheer about, too. The Cold War ended with the collapse of the Soviet Union. The U.S. and its allies drove aggressor Saddam Hussein out of Kuwait. The stock market rose to new highs. Americans led the way into the new world of the Internet and the World Wide Web. And despite the fears of many, the world's computer systems did not crash on the final night of the decade, as 1999 gave way to the year 2000 and a new century.

Buzz Lightyear from *Toy Story.*

- **The U.S. population** is now almost 250 million, an increase of 9.8% since the 1980 census.

- **Saddam Hussein**, the dictator of Iraq, invades and annexes the small, oil-rich nation of Kuwait. America and the United Nations demand that he remove his troops.

- **West and East Germany**, divided into two separate countries since the end of World War II, are reunited as one nation.

- **Movie audiences** flock to *Ghost*, *Home Alone*, and *Pretty Woman*, which makes Julia Roberts a major star.

- A Congressional committee reports that **Americans spend more than 30 billion dollars** each year on weight-loss programs and products, many of which are useless.

Nelson Mandela, an opponent of racial segregation (apartheid), is released from a South African jail after 27 years; he visits the U.S. and receives a warm welcome.

1991

In **Operation Desert Storm**, U.S. and United Nations troops force Saddam Hussein's army out of Kuwait, bombard Iraq, and destroy the Iraqi army, but do not attempt to take control of Iraq.

- In April, the **Dow-Jones Industrial Average closes** above 3,000 for the first time.

- Serial murderer **Jeffrey Dahmer**, who killed 17 men and boys over a 13-year period, is arrested in Milwaukee when an intended victim escapes and alerts police.

- The **Soviet Union collapses** as its "socialist republics" declare themselves to be independent nations.

- **Bobby Bonilla of baseball's New York Mets** becomes the highest paid professional athlete; his new contract will pay him 29 million dollars over 5 years.

U.S. Marines Field Hospital with supplies, in the Saudi Arabian Desert.

1992

- A speeding car driven by **Rodney King**, an African-American, is stopped by Los Angeles police, who beat King with batons. When the policemen are tried, a jury finds them not guilty and riots break out throughout the city. The result is 53 deaths and a billion dollars in damages.

- A basketball "**dream team**" of NBA stars, including Michael Jordan, Larry Bird, Magic Johnson, David Robinson, and Charles Barkley represent the U.S. at the Summer Olympics in Korea and easily win the gold medal.

- The **giant Mall of America** opens in Minnesota. It will grow to contain more than 500 stores and employ over 12,000 people. Some 40 million shoppers will visit it each year.

- The **AIDS** epidemic in the U.S. peaks as 78,000 new cases are diagnosed this year.

Bill Clinton, a Democrat from Arkansas, wins the presidential election in a three-man race against incumbent George H. W. Bush and third-party candidate H. Ross Perot.

1993

Ty Inc. introduces the first nine of many **Beanie Babies**, animals stuffed with plastic pellets, or "beans." The toys will become a national craze as collectors strive to own all of them.

- The African-American writer **Toni Morrison**, author of *Beloved* and *Song of Solomon*, wins the Nobel Prize for Literature.

- A **bomb explodes in the car park** beneath one of the towers of the World Trade Center in New York City, killing six people and injuring hundreds. Six Islamic fundamentalists are arrested for the crime.

- Near Waco, Texas, **FBI agents attack the compound of the Branch Davidian Seventh Day Adventists**, a sect suspected of stockpiling weapons and of child abuse. The compound bursts into flames and 76 sect members die, including David Koresh, the leader.

U.S. troops participate in a U.N. effort to **end starvation** in the African nation of Somalia. But warfare among Somali factions plunges the country into chaos and results in the deaths of many Americans. The U.S. will withdraw early next year.

1994

- Major League **baseball players go on strike** in August; the season ends and the World Series is canceled.

- The hospital drama **"ER"** debuts on NBC. An instant hit, it will run for 15 seasons and win a record 124 Emmy nominations.

- A **major earthquake** strikes California's San Fernando Valley. Roadways and buildings collapse, killing 57 people.

- The national election gives Republicans, who presented voters a **"Contract with America,"** control of both houses of Congress for the first time in 40 years.

- Moviegoers around the world are delighted by the film **Forrest Gump**, which will win Oscars for Best Picture and Best Actor for its star Tom Hanks.

BK 4 0 1 3 9 7 0   06 17 94

Former football star **O.J. Simpson**, fleeing in a white Ford Bronco, tries to escape police who want to arrest him for the murder of his wife, Nicole Simpson, and her friend, Ron Goldman. Millions watch the chase on television. Simpson is apprehended and jailed.

1995

A truck containing a **fertilizer bomb** explodes at the Murrah Federal Building in Oklahoma City, causing massive damage to the building and its day-care center. The aftermath is pictured on left, where a shell of a car sits in front of the building after the explosion. Among the 168 dead are 19 children. Timothy McVeigh and Terry Nichols are arrested for the crime.

- The **O.J. Simpson trial** goes on for more than nine months before the jury finds Simpson not guilty; an estimated 150 million people watch the verdict on television.

- The **average American income is** $35,900 a year. A gallon of gas costs $1.09. Eggs are 87 cents a dozen and coffee costs $4.07 a pound.

- **eBay**, the online auction site, is founded in California.

Pixar Studios and Disney release *Toy Story*, the first full-length film that is completely computer-animated. **Buzz Lightyear**, a main character from the movie, will become a hot toy.

1996

- **America's women gymnasts** win the team gold medal at the Summer Olympics in Atlanta.

- **Welfare reform legislation is enacted**, fulfilling President Clinton's campaign pledge to "end welfare as we know it."

- The hunt for a terrorist known as the **Unabomber**, who has killed three people and wounded 22 with bombs sent to them through the mail, ends with the arrest of recluse Ted Kaczynski.

- Scientists announce the **cloning of a sheep**, Dolly, the first mammal cloned from a cell from an adult animal.

President Clinton is re-elected, (with Vice President Al Gore, right) defeating Republican Bob Dole and Reform Party candidate H. Ross Perot.

1997

Great Britain's Princess Diana, 36-year-old ex-wife of the Prince of Wales, is killed in a car crash in Paris.

- James Cameron's film *Titanic*, starring Leonardo DiCaprio and Kate Winslet as lovers aboard the doomed ocean liner, is released. It becomes the highest grossing film in history to date, taking in 1.8 billion dollars worldwide.

- **Madeleine Albright** is sworn in as the first woman Secretary of State.

- In a civil suit filed by the families of Nicole Simpson and Ron Goldman, the jury finds **O. J. Simpson** responsible for their murders. He is ordered to pay 8.5 million dollars in compensatory damages.

- **J. K. Rowling's** first Harry Potter book is published in the U.K. under the title *Harry Potter and the Philosopher's Stone*. It will be published in the U.S. the next year as *Harry Potter and the Sorcerer's Stone*.

1998

- Revelations of **improper relations** between President Clinton and White House intern Monica Lewinsky, and Clinton's denial of the affair before a grand jury, lead to his impeachment by the House of Representatives.

- Some 76 million people tune in for the final episode of the popular TV comedy series "**Seinfeld**," the self-described "show about nothing."

- The drug Sildenafil, marketed by Pfizer as **Viagra**, goes on sale as a treatment for erectile dysfunction; it soon will achieve annual sales of more than a billion dollars.

- A new company, **Google, Inc.**, is founded by two Stanford University graduate students.

The U.S. women's hockey team and 15-year-old figure skater **Tara Lapinski** are among the gold medalists at the Winter Olympics in Japan.

1999

- **President Clinton's impeachment trial** in the Senate ends with the President's acquittal.

- **Two teenage boys open fire at Columbine High School** near Denver, killing 12 students and one teacher before committing suicide.

- **John F. Kennedy Jr.**, his wife, and his sister-in-law are killed when the small plane he is piloting crashes into the ocean off Martha's Vineyard, Massachusetts.

- The **Pokemon** (a contraction of Pocket Monsters) craze sweeps the U.S., as kids clamor for cards, video games, toys, and TV shows featuring the many Pokemon "species."

- **Cost of a new house** averages 132 thousand, a gallon of gas costs $1.22, and a loaf of bread is $1.49.

- As the new century approaches, businesses and governments worry about the so-called **Y2K, or millennium bug.** They work to re-program the world's computers so they won't fail at midnight on New Year's Eve when the date changes from 1999 to 2000. No outages were reported, and the whole world goes on with its normal life as the **20th century comes to an end**.

Picture Credits